Self-Est

Looking Up Instead of
Looking Inside

Leslie Vernick

New
Growth
Press
WWW.NEWGROWTHPRESS.COM

New Growth Press, Greensboro, NC 27404
www.newgrowthpress.com

Unless otherwise indicated, all Scripture quotations are taken from the Holy Bible, New Living Translation, copyright © 1996, 2004, 2007 by Tyndale House Foundation. Used by permission of Tyndale House Publishers, Inc., Carol Stream, Illinois 60188. All rights reserved.

Scripture quotations marked ESV are taken from *The Holy Bible, English Standard Version.* Copyright © 2000; 2001 by Crossway Bibles, a division of Good News Publishers. Used by permission. All rights reserved.

Cover Design: Tandem Creative, Tom Temple, tandem creative.net; Typesetting: Lisa Parnell, lparnell.com

ISBN: 978-1-942572-49-7 (Print)
ISBN: 978-1-942572-50-3 (eBook)

Library of Congress Cataloging-in-Publication Data
    Names: Vernick, Leslie, author.
    Title: Self-esteem : looking up instead of looking inside / Leslie Vernick.
    Description: Greensboro, NC : New Growth Press, 2016.
    Identifiers: LCCN 2015042166 | ISBN 9781942572497 (print) | ISBN 9781942572503 (ebook)
    Subjects: LCSH: Self-esteem—Religious aspects—Christianity.
    Classification: LCC BV4647.S43 V47 2016 | DDC 248.4—dc23
    LC record available at http://lccn.loc.gov/2015042166

Printed in China

23 22 21 20 19 18 17 16   1 2 3 4 5

As a child, I never liked being me. I believed that I wasn't pretty enough, smart enough, popular enough, or skinny enough. In elementary school I was never invited to birthday parties for the popular girls in my school, and I was often the last one picked for kickball team. Therapists would say I struggled with a poor self-image and low self-esteem.

When I was eight years old, my world turned upside down. My mother decided she no longer wanted to be married to my father and my parents went through an ugly divorce. My mother moved us to an apartment in Chicago where I knew no one. Broken families were rare when I was a child, and I felt ashamed and self-conscious.

In my child's mind, I thought if I could copy one of the more popular girls' laugh, look, or mannerism, then the kids at school would like me. The odds were against me fitting in. I came from a broken family, had a face full of freckles, two chipped front teeth, and a haircut that my mother gave me while she was drinking and in a bad mood.

You might have had a hard childhood too, but as adult women we often still struggle with these issues, don't we? We compare and contrast our lives and our thighs and feel inferior. We don't like ourselves. We have an internal voice that reminds us we're never good enough, pretty enough, thin enough, spiritual enough, organized enough, loving enough, smart enough, or successful enough.

Ann Voskamp, the author of the book *One Thousand Gifts*, writes, "I wake to the discontent of life in my skin. I wake to self-hatred. To the wrestle to get

3

it all done, the restless anxiety that I am failing, always failing. I live tired, afraid, anxious, weary. Would I ever be enough, find enough, do enough?"[1]

Most women I know and work with struggle in some way with this internal feeling of not being enough. Let's look at where it originates.

Identity Is Always Forged in Relationship

God designed the human spirit to connect with other humans. Studies on newborns demonstrate that when they are shown colorful pictures—a bright red ball, a yellow block, a beautiful flower—and a human face, they will always look toward the face. From the start of life a baby naturally gazes into her mother's eyes asking the question, *Who am I?*

Ideally during the mother-child interaction, the baby begins to get a sense of herself as someone who is loved, protected, valued, provided for, enjoyed, and important. This is God's plan for babies—to experience unconditional love from both mother and father, which sets the stage for understanding God's love for them. This helps the infant start life with a secure sense of herself. She feels in the core of her being that she is enough to receive unconditional love and acceptance, even if she cries and keeps her parents up all night, throws up on them, and is cranky.

Sadly, many babies do not get this kind of unconditional love and acceptance. Her parent(s) may be exhausted, caring for other children, working full-time, or taking care of elderly parents. Mom and/or dad may be distracted with texting, e-mails, Facebook, or other interests. Her parents may be drug addicted, immature, having marital problems, depressed, or checked out. And even the best parents get tired, blow it, and act sinfully. No child escapes family life without a few nicks to their self-image and self-esteem.

In addition to the parents' role, our sense of self continues to be shaped as we interact with siblings, schoolmates, friends, and sports teammates, learning new skills and becoming more aware of the world around us. We gaze into the eyes of other people, such as teachers, coaches, friends, boyfriends, mentors, husbands, and bosses and ask the question, *Who do you say I am?*

Sharon is one example. She grew up in a loving home and felt confident and secure at ten years old. However, when her father lost his job and her mom started working full-time to help support the family, she could no longer be homeschooled. She started sixth grade at the public school, where her peers were a group of mean girls who teased and laughed at her throughout junior high. Although Sharon's mom visited the principal in an effort to remedy this, the girls continued to subtly ridicule and reject Sharon.

Being bullied is a horrible experience, but Sharon began to identify with what the girls were saying about her. She began to believe she *was* ugly, fat, stupid, a loser, and an undesirable person, friend, and girl. The bullies affected not only how Sharon felt, but also how she saw herself. This shift in her self-image had a huge impact on Sharon's self-esteem, and she began her high school years feeling insecure and believing she was not good at anything.

In high school, her physical education teacher noticed that Sharon was an exceptionally fast runner. She suggested that Sharon try out for the track team and she put in a good word for her with the coach. Sharon made the team and excelled.

By the end of high school, Sharon had set the school record in the 50-yard dash and received an athletic scholarship to a top university. Sharon made a few good friends in high school and was asked to her senior prom by one of the most popular guys in school. During high school Sharon's sense of herself shifted again. She saw herself differently and, as a result, she felt more confident, competent, and valuable.

Later, during her junior year of college, Sharon seriously injured her knee in an automobile accident and could no longer compete in track. She lost her scholarship, and that nagging feeling that she was not enough returned.

Whether we succeed or fail, are popular or rejected, when we base our value and worth on external sources rather than what God says, our self-image will shift like sand, leading to an unstable and anxious sense of who we are.

If you find yourself in that place, don't beat yourself up. The Bible warns us that we automatically and unconsciously exchange the truth of God for a lie (Romans 1:25). In addition, it says that we naturally worship the creation rather than our Creator (Romans 1:23). What that means is that we all listen to false voices and build our identity on shaky foundations rather than on what God says. Whether we think too highly of ourselves or we don't think enough of ourselves, we all need healing in order to see ourselves truthfully—as God sees us.

Remember, although God designated parents to give their child her initial sense of who she is, ultimately, if we are to grow strong and secure in who we are, our Creator must have the final word. He is the only one who knows fully who we are and who we were made to become. He's the only one who will always tell us the truth, who will never change, and who loves us unconditionally all the time.

Instead of looking to God to tell us who we are, as fallen human beings we seek external sources to tell us who we are. When we do that, instead of feeling secure and loved, we become self-conscious, self-focused, self-centered, and self-absorbed.

Six False Voices We Allow to Define Our Value and Worth

As a Christian counselor and coach, I've worked with hundreds, if not thousands, of women to transform a negative self-image. But I also had to do the hard work myself to see myself differently (self-image), and to feel differently inside (self-esteem).

Following are six areas where people seek their sense of worth and value: popularity, performance, possessions, power, position, and perfectionism. On the surface, they don't look sinful or harmful. However, when we depend on them to define us, we will be deceived, confused, and anxious because they are shaky foundations on which to base our identity, value, and worth. When we listen to these voices, we forfeit the opportunity to grow into the women God has created us to become.

Popularity

For a long time I believed I wasn't *enough* because I wasn't popular with my peers. I longed to be liked, accepted, and valued by others. I believed that if I got invited to certain birthday parties or was picked first for the kickball team, that would mean I made it. I was good enough, I was worth something.

When I didn't get what my heart craved, I came unglued. I felt worthless, unloved, and hopeless. My internal sense of who I was depended on whether or not the people in my world liked and valued me. When they did, it felt great. When they didn't, I grew despondent. I've learned that depending on others to define me is a scary and an unstable place to rest my self-worth.

Don't misunderstand me. There is nothing sinful or wrong with desiring acceptance and love. It's a fundamental desire for us all. I still prefer popularity to rejection, and I know I'm not alone. My problem was not my desire, but that I depended on sinful, fallible human beings to give me something only God can give me fully.

After Jesus healed a deaf man the crowd said, "Everything he does is wonderful" (Mark 7:37). But just a few chapters earlier, Jesus's own family said, "He's out of his mind" (Mark 3:21). In addition, the most influential people in Jesus's crowd, the teachers of the religious law, said about Jesus, "He's possessed by Satan" (Mark 3:22).

Which was true? Among all the voices that tell us who we are, how do we discern who or what to believe? Although I imagine those comments hurt Jesus, he did not allow them to define his personhood. Jesus knew who he was and his identity wasn't based on the words of others, but on the words of his Father. God said, "You are my dearly loved Son, and you bring me great joy" (Luke 3:22).

Depending on popularity or the approval of others to define who you are turns you into a people pleaser and not a God pleaser. That keeps you from growing into the woman God made you to be.

Performance

Are you the kind of woman who feels good about yourself when you get it all done? When you check everything off your list? When you succeed in accomplishing a tough task? It's a great feeling, isn't it? But what happens inside you when you're sick or tired, and you can't do it all? What happens inside you when you make a huge mistake, or your list goes on and on and there is no end? What does it say about who you are when you don't get everything done?

Not a thing—unless you define yourself by your performance and your worth depends on your ability to accomplish and perform. Then you will feel worthless and shamed about your inability to get it all done.

Paul tells us that from his prison cell, a place of nonproductivity, he learned some valuable spiritual lessons. He reminds us of all he accomplished, all he did as a religious Jewish Pharisee, yet he concludes by saying, "But now I consider them worthless because of what Christ has done. Yes, everything is worthless when compared with the infinite value of knowing Christ Jesus my Lord. For his sake I have discarded everything else, counting it all as garbage, so that I could gain Christ and become one with him" (Philippians 3:7–9a). You can read the entire book of Philippians to see what Paul learned in prison when he was stopped from doing anything "productive."

Paul saw himself differently when he didn't depend on his performance—good or bad—to define who he was. Breaking free from the internal demands to do more gives us precious time to discover more of who God is and who he made us to be. If or when God puts us in a season of nonproductivity, it does not mean we're failing or worthless. We are more than what we accomplish each day.

Possessions

I know a woman who describes everything she owns by the brand. She says things like, "I just bought a new BMW." Or "I love Kate Spade purses." Or "I'm so happy my husband bought me a Rolex watch for my birthday." I think she is trying to say to herself and others that because she owns these things, she must be attractive, worthy, special, or valuable.

Please don't misunderstand what I am saying. I enjoy owning nice things too. But having them (or not having them) does not define me or change the way I feel about myself. I am the same person in Target workout clothes as I am in Nike gear. Having nice things is not a statement about me or you.

If you're not sure whether you're stuck in this lie, ask yourself if you overspend on things you don't need just to feel better about yourself. Do you have far more stuff than you use or need but have a hard time getting rid of it? If so, it might be a sign that you use possessions as a status symbol to feel like you are enough. And the lack of possessions can produce the feeling that you are not enough. You tell yourself that you're not as good as the woman who has more.

I remember a friend who didn't invite anyone over for dinner because her house was not as nice or big as that of others in our small group. We loved her. We didn't care about the size of her house, but she cared. She allowed her house to define her worth and make her feel "less than" or "not enough."

If you are reading this and have embraced a minimalist lifestyle, you may still allow possessions to define you. You tell yourself that you are doing it right by not having stuff. You are more worthy, more special, more godly than the woman who clings to her stuff.

The apostle Paul tells us that he learned to be content living with plenty and living with very little. Possessions are for us to enjoy, but they can also encumber us. They are never meant to define us. Marketers would have you believe that you are worth more if you purchase their goods. Next time you watch television commercials, listen carefully. The tagline in most advertising is, "you deserve it and are worth it." They promise us worthiness if we buy what they sell. But don't fall for it. At best it's a temporary fix, but soon you're off to the mall for the next thing you need to buy in order to feel like you're enough.

Power

Everyone wants some power in life. At a minimum, we want the power to choose our own way, to decide what we will say yes to and what we will say no to. Even toddlers fight for that power when they shut their mouth tight and refuse to eat something they don't like.

No one likes feeling helpless and powerless. However, when having power defines us as powerful, we are often tempted to misuse that power—whether it is political, physical, sexual, economic, or spiritual power—to bully and manipulate others so that we can control the situation and get what we want.

Jesus warns those with power not to misuse it to boost their self-esteem or serve themselves. He tells his disciples,

> "You know that those who are considered rulers of the Gentiles lord it over them, and their great ones exercise authority over them. But it shall not be so among you. But whoever would be great among you must be your servant, and whoever would be first among you must be slave of all." (Mark 10:42–44 ESV)

Being powerful, just like being wealthy or popular, does not define you as a good person or more deserving or worthy than someone who does not have power. Adolf Hitler, the German chancellor during World War II, was powerful and popular, but he used his power and popularity for evil purposes. As women we can use our sexual power over men to feel worthy, attractive, and loved.

Power, like popularity and possessions, often distracts us from God and can corrupt our hearts and minds. We get deceived into believing that our power, popularity, performance, and even possessions come from our own strengths. We believe that we are enough and don't need God. We refuse to acknowledge that everything good in us is from God and if he's given us a position of power, we should use it wisely for his purposes.

And those who feel powerless—the weak, the helpless, the disenfranchised victims of the powerful—often feel like God doesn't see or care about their plight. They believe they are not worthy to be cherished and protected. That's not true. God says he sees what's happening and will bring them justice and comfort. (See for example, Psalm 9:9–10 and Psalm 10, especially verses 14–18).

Position

Power and position often go together; if I'm the president of a company, country, or leader in an organization, then that must mean I'm wise and competent. That might be true, or it might not be. Your professional position is only one part of who you are. You still have weaknesses. There are sinful parts of yourself that are also parts of who you are. These too must be acknowledged if you are to be a whole person and have a truthful self-image.

Those who achieve power in high positions never feel secure. Even a dictator knows that things can suddenly change with a shift of allegiance. That's why dictators use power in sinful ways to secure their positions. Their popularity doesn't hold them there.

As soon as someone else becomes more powerful, they too will be ousted.

Some women feel inferior or not enough because they do not have a desired position. If you are not a wife or a mother, you may allow your lack of having this position to tell you that there must be something wrong with you. You believe you're not pretty enough, thin enough, emotionally mature enough, or spiritual enough to have that role. But that's not true. Look around the next time you go to the shopping mall. Is every wife or mother thin, beautiful, mature, or spiritual? Not at my mall.

God knows you desire those things, and your desires are good. But just as I desired popularity as a child and yet didn't receive it, there are times we don't get everything we desire. It hurts us, but it is not a statement about who you are or who you are not. Never confuse your pain with your value or identity.

Perfectionism

Perfectionism comes from an internal voice that constantly tells you that if you're not perfect, you can't possibly be enough or loved. Everyone else can be a sinner and still be loved, but not you. Everyone else can have weaknesses and be accepted, but not you. Everyone else can make a mistake and receive grace and forgiveness, but not you.

Even if you have people in your life who actually love you and accept you, you don't receive it because all you can see is your flaws, sins, mistakes, and failures. You put yourself in a no-win position with this mindset. The only way you can feel good about being you is to achieve the impossible. You must be perfect.

When you fail, which you always will, the result is shame, self-hatred, and despair.

How do you know if you're caught in this lie? Listen to your internal self-talk when you mess up. Does it sound something like this: "I can't believe I said that. What's wrong with me?" In other words, you're never allowed to say something stupid or sinful or make a mistake. Or perhaps you say, "I just can't forgive myself. I can't believe I even did such a horrible thing." Why do you have a hard time accepting that you are a finite, fallible human being? Why not accept that you are a sinner and capable of doing sinful things?

It's because you expect yourself to be better than that. You expect yourself to be perfect.

Healing from a Damaged Self-Image

The answer to healing a negative self-image and low self-esteem is not trying harder to be enough. It's not found in trying to get more of anything. A healthy sense of self doesn't happen by focusing on ourselves at all. All those paths either lead to pride or more shame and fear because we fail to measure up.

If you become aware of sinful patterns in your life, or some internal weaknesses that you need to work on, I hope you ask God for forgiveness for Jesus's sake and then ask him for the Spirit's help to change. But understand this important truth: you will never get to a place where you don't see your sins and your weaknesses. And after all your hard work at self-improvement, by whose yardstick will you measure whether you are finally good enough, worthy enough, or acceptable enough? If it is your own yardstick or some other fallible human's yardstick, you will never have the stability and security your heart craves. Nor will you have a truthful and healthy sense of who you are.

Friend, God has something much better for you.

A Biblical Case Study

Let's look at a woman who did not feel good about herself. She knew full well that she was not enough and could never be enough. She had five failed marriages and the man she was living with was not her husband. She was an unpopular woman—the women of her community shunned her. She was a Samaritan, and the Jews despised the Samaritans and saw them as inferior. She was a woman who had no power or position because of her gender, her marital status, and her race.

Let's see how a single encounter with Jesus changed the way she saw herself. (See John 4:3–42 for the full story.) Jesus met this woman at the community water well. She went there all alone that day to draw her daily supply of water. In New Testament Middle Eastern culture, women went to the well with other women in the early morning before it got too hot. Being there alone at noon tells us how utterly unloved and alone she was.

While at the well she noticed a Jewish man sitting nearby. He startled her by speaking to her, asking for a drink of water. This was highly irregular. Jewish people did not talk to Samaritans. They considered them garbage. Not only that, but she was a Samaritan *woman* and he was a Jewish *man*—another reason for him not to speak to her. Jesus violated cultural practice by asking her for a drink and engaging in a lengthy conversation with her. During their talk, he even offered her a valuable gift, living water.

Jesus engaged with this woman, talking theology, talking about life and relationships, and talking about God. He revealed to her something he had rarely shared publicly. He told her he was the Jewish Messiah. He never focused on her flaws and failures, though he was well aware of them. He saw beyond her gender, her race, her status, and her messed-up life. He saw the woman he created her to be. As Jesus talked with her, the woman asked him questions and Jesus took time to answer them.

In her conversation with Jesus, the woman began to see herself differently. She was no longer just an unloved, unimportant, immoral, Samaritan woman. She was a person in a life-changing conversation with someone who claimed to be the long-awaited Jewish Messiah. This amazing man knew every bad thing about her, yet he didn't treat her with contempt or indifference, but with dignity and respect. Their conversation brought out sides of her that she had long forgotten—her curiosity, inquisitiveness, theological questions, and hunger for truth.

She began to see herself as Jesus saw her—valuable and loved by him. Her identity went beyond what she did or didn't do, how she felt, what others thought about her, or even what she thought about herself. Those things no longer defined her.

She realized in her core that she was more than her race, her gender, her education, or her past. She was set free from who she thought she was and from what other people told her she was. She was free to become the woman God made her to be.

The remarkable thing about this story is its ending. This woman's countenance was so transformed that when she ran back into her town shouting, "Come and see a man who told me everything I ever did," people listened to her. The same people who regularly scorned and rejected her noticed something different about this woman. The Bible tells us that many people came to Christ because of her words (John 4:39–42).

We Are Changed by How We See God

We've already seen that identity is forged and formed in relationship. From infancy we need assurance that we are deeply loved and accepted in spite of our flaws, weakness, and sins. We've already learned that this rock-solid assurance can never fully come from our family of origin or our own strength, striving to be enough. It won't come from our own popularity, performance, possessions, power, position, or perfection, which are always too unstable to give us what our heart craves. It also can't come from other people, who sometimes fail us and let us down. It can only come from the One who is perfect. The One who knows us perfectly and loves us ferociously and unconditionally. It can only come from God.

Like the woman at the well, we need a personal encounter with Jesus. The psalmist writes, "He sent out his word and healed them" (Psalm 107:20). Jesus is the living Word of God (John 1:14). Who does he say that you are? This shift—from looking to ourselves or to others to define us is crucial to our healing. The Bible tells us, "For you are the fountain of life, the light by which we see" (Psalm 36:9). We only see ourselves clearly when we're looking at God and not at ourselves.

Psychologist David Benner says, "Genuine self-knowledge begins by looking at God and noticing how God is looking at us. Grounding our knowing of our self in God's knowing of us anchors us in reality. It also anchors us in God."[2]

C. S. Lewis writes, "How God thinks of us is not only more important [than how we think of him], but infinitely more important."[3] Let's look at a few passages in Scripture that help us see how God thinks of us.

> When I look at the night sky and see the work of your fingers—the moon and the stars you set in place—what are mere mortals that you should think about them, human beings that you should care for them? Yet you made them only a little lower than God and crowned them with glory and honor. You gave them charge of everything you made, putting all things under their authority. (Psalm 8:3–6)

> O LORD, you have examined my heart and know everything about me. You know when I sit down or stand up. You know my thoughts even when I'm far away. . . . I can never escape from your Spirit! I can never get away from your presence! . . . You made all the delicate, inner parts of my body and knit me together in my mother's womb. . . . You saw me before I was born. Every

day of my life was recorded in your book. . . . How precious are your thoughts about me, O God. They cannot be numbered! I can't even count them; they outnumber the grains of sand! And when I wake up, you are still with me! . . . Point out anything in me that offends you, and lead me along the path of everlasting life. (Psalm 139)

For while we were still weak *[not enough]*, at the right time Christ died for the ungodly. For one will scarcely die for a righteous person— though perhaps for a good person one would dare even to die—but God shows his love for us in that while we were still sinners, Christ died for us. (Romans 5:6–8 ESV, brackets added)

Even before he made the world, God loved us and chose us in Christ to be holy and without fault in his eyes. God decided in advance to adopt us into his own family by bringing us to himself through Jesus Christ. This is what he wanted to do, and it gave him great pleasure. (Ephesians 1:4–5)

Perhaps you've read these passages before and nothing inside has changed. You still feel unworthy, unloved, not enough. You might be thinking, *I've already tried looking at what God says, but it didn't work.* Let me provide the missing piece.

Knowing the Truth Isn't Believing the Truth

When you read what God says in the Bible, are they words on a page or do you take them into your heart and believe him? Most of us don't need more informational truth about God or what he says, but we do need more transformational truth. That comes when we not only listen to what God says, but we see it as crucial to our well-being and believe it with our hearts.

Imagine that you receive a registered letter. You open it and read that you have inherited ten million dollars from a recently deceased relative whom you don't remember. The law firm that sent the letter would like you to get in touch with them immediately.

How would you feel? It depends on whether you believed the letter was genuine or fake. If you didn't believe it, there would be no change in you. You would laugh or be upset, and you would throw the letter away instead of feeling like a millionaire. However, if you believed it, if you discovered it was true, it would definitely change you. You would begin to feel differently, think differently, and live differently.

The Bible tells us that it's unbelief rather than a lack of knowledge that keeps us from experiencing the truth of what God says. Satan knows a lot of true things about God, but he doesn't believe. Learning the truth won't change us, but believing it does.

Jesus told his followers that the *work* God desires is for us to believe (John 6:28–29). Jesus knows that there will always be a struggle within us to trust and believe what God says over all the noise and lies in our own head. Jesus also warned his followers that Satan is a liar who continually tries to confuse us about what is true about God, ourselves, and how life really works (John 8:44). If we're not mindful of his strategies, we will easily fall for his lies. One of the biggest lies he tells us is that we can be enough without God or that *feeling* worthy enough or good enough is crucial for a healthy self-image and positive self-esteem.

On the contrary, God says that believing him and abiding or resting in what he says is the secret to transformative change. The Bible tells us, "I the LORD speak the truth; I declare what is right" (Isaiah 45:19 ESV). Jesus tells us, "My sheep hear my voice" (John 10:27 ESV). Over seventy times in the Gospels Jesus says, "I tell you the truth." Jesus doesn't just want us to believe in him, he wants us to believe him.

The apostle John knew the path to change when he wrote the following:

> So we have come to know and *to believe* the love that God has for us. God is love, and whoever abides in love abides in God, and God abides in him. By this is love perfected with us, so that we may have confidence for the day of judgment, because as he is so also are we in this world. There is no fear in love, but perfect love casts out fear. For fear has to do with punishment, and whoever fears has not been perfected in love. (1 John 4:16–18 ESV, italics added)

When we know and rest in God's unconditional love and acceptance for us, we are free to let go of our fear that we are not enough. His love for you and me does not depend upon whether we are enough or not. His love is a free gift, not something we earn or deserve. What a relief! If we can't earn it and don't deserve it, we can never lose it. God's love for us is not dependent on us at all.

Friend, you change the way you see yourself and feel about yourself when you believe and abide in the truth of what God says about you. The hard work is not in changing yourself, striving to be enough, but in believing what God says. Once you believe, the remainder of the change comes naturally.

I want you to begin today to speak God's truth to yourself.

- *I have value and worth to God.* (Matthew 10:31; 12:12)
- *I am deeply and fully loved by God.* (John 17:23; Romans 5:8; 8:31–39)
- *I am forgiven and given a clean slate by God, who desires to bring me into a close relationship with him.* (Psalm 103:8–12; John 5:24; Acts 3:19; 13:38–39; Ephesians 1:7; Colossians 1:13–14)
- *I belong to him; he adopts me into his family.* (John 14:18; Romans 8:15–17; Galatians 4:6–7; Ephesians 1:4–5; 1 John 3:1)
- *My life has meaning and purpose. I am not an accident.* (John 15:9; Romans 5:10–11; 8:1–39; 1 Corinthians 1:8; Ephesians 2:4–10)

Remember, the lies we've believed for so long often have deep roots and are not removed all at once. God's Word tells us that we change by renewing our mind (Romans 12:2). Therefore it's critical that we practice speaking the truth to ourselves, so that we don't forget who we really are (Colossians 1:13–23).

Mother Theresa famously said, "Knowledge of God gives love and knowledge of self gives humility." Humility is the outcome of having a healthy self-image and good self-esteem. We look to Christ and not to the world, others, or ourselves to tell us who we are. All that is good in us is from God and for his glory. When we rest in that place, we're neither fearful nor proud; rather, we're grateful and secure.

We press on to know this amazing God who loves us so much that he empowers us through his Son Jesus to live a life beyond pleasing or fulfilling ourselves. It is only from that place that we can know that we are enough. And from that place we can love others deeply, find meaning, and live each day on purpose.

Endnotes

1. Ann Voskamp, *One Thousand Gifts* (Grand Rapids: Zondervan, 2010), 27.

2. David Benner, *The Gift of Being Yourself: The Sacred Call to Self-Discovery* (Westmont, IL: IVP Books, 2004), 48.

3. C. S. Lewis, "The Weight of Glory," in *The Weight of Glory: And Other Addresses* (New York: HarperCollins, 2001), 38.